A is for Artisanal

An Alphabet Book for the Hip, Modern Baby

Written by Matthew Goldenberg   *Illustrated by Benjamin Schwartz*

A is for Artisanal: An Alphabet Book for the Hip, Modern Baby

Published by Paradisiac Publishing. http://www.theparadisiacgroup.com. No part of this book may be reproduced without expressed written permission of the author, illustrator, or publisher, except for brief quotes for review purposes.

ISBN: 978--0--9853168--5--3

Ava adores artisanal asiago.

Bjorn is brought to brunch in a Bob.

Bob is brought to brunch in a Bjorn.

C

aleb crushes the chin-up challenge at CrossFit.

D aniel devours documentaries
on the Discovery Channel.

Emma
enjoys eating
edamame.

Fiona finds fresh fruit at the farmers' market.

Gavin greedily gorges
on Greek goodness.

H

enry hops into his hybrid hatchback.

I

sabella interfaces with ingenious individuals on her iPad.

Jack
jocularly
jabs like
Jon Stewart.

K

evin knows the keel of his kayak is Kevlar.

L iam loves lapping up lattes.

Madeleine marvels at the Montessori method.

N
oah needs nightly news
from NPR.

O

livia only orders organic olive oil.

P arker's preferred potent potable is postprandial port.

Quinn questions the quality of the quinoa from Quito.

Rory rummages through rubbish, reclaiming reusable refuse to recycle.

S ophie sears salmon
    in her stainless steel smoker.

Theo triumphs

in the tortuous, torturous triathlon.

Uma is a Unitarian Universalist:

understanding
and urbane
or uppity and
ungodly?

Vincent the vegetarian values verdant victuals.

Willa whoops wildly while watching the Women's World Cup.

X

ander's Xmas:
   an Xbox, a xylophone and XM radio.

Yoshi yearns for youth yoga.

Zoey zooms, zigs and zags

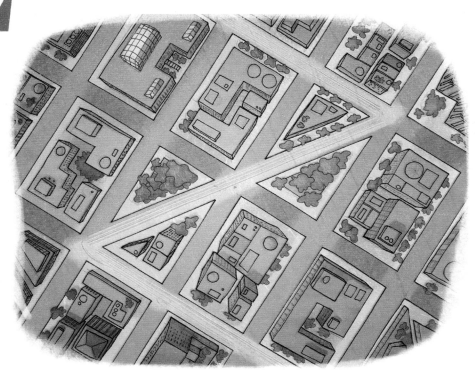

in her Zipcar.

About Matthew Goldenberg:

Birmingham-born, Matthew is a practicing psychiatrist, language lover, football fan and avuncular adorer of two terrific tots. He's lived in several hip places including Chapel Hill, NC, Washington, DC and London, UK.

About Benjamin Schwartz:

A dedicated doodler, humane humorist and enthusiastic eater of pies, Benjamin loves creating comic content for cool kids. His cartoons appear in "The New Yorker"; his physical being appears in New York.

24223477R00018

Made in the USA
Lexington, KY
10 July 2013